ACTIVITIES

FACTS

Handy hints and tips

Congratulations on having your very own set of *Hieroglyph It!* stencils. The mysterious secrets of Ancient Egypt will soon become clear to you!

But first you must practice drawing good glyphs. Hold the stencil down on your paper firmly with one hand. Draw against the edge to make an outline, or color in the shape first. Whichever you choose, be sure not to let the stencil move.

Carved hands from the temple of the pharaoh Ramesses II, The Great. He reigned for 67 years, died at age 92 and had more than 100 children!

Using your stencils

You can turn your stencils over to make the shapes face the other way. Outlines are easy, but what about filling them in? Find your shape on the color guide and then you can copy the details onto your drawing.

A cartouche was the special shape used to frame the names of kings and queens. Use the straight edges and corners of your stencil to help you draw one.

Ancient effects

Here are one or two tricks to give your glyphs a very ancient look, just like the real thing.

You will need:
wax crayons, colored pencils and felt-tip pens,
strong, thin paper...

...brick, wood, cloth, or other textured surfaces.

① Lay a sheet of paper over the textured surface. Put the stencil on top.

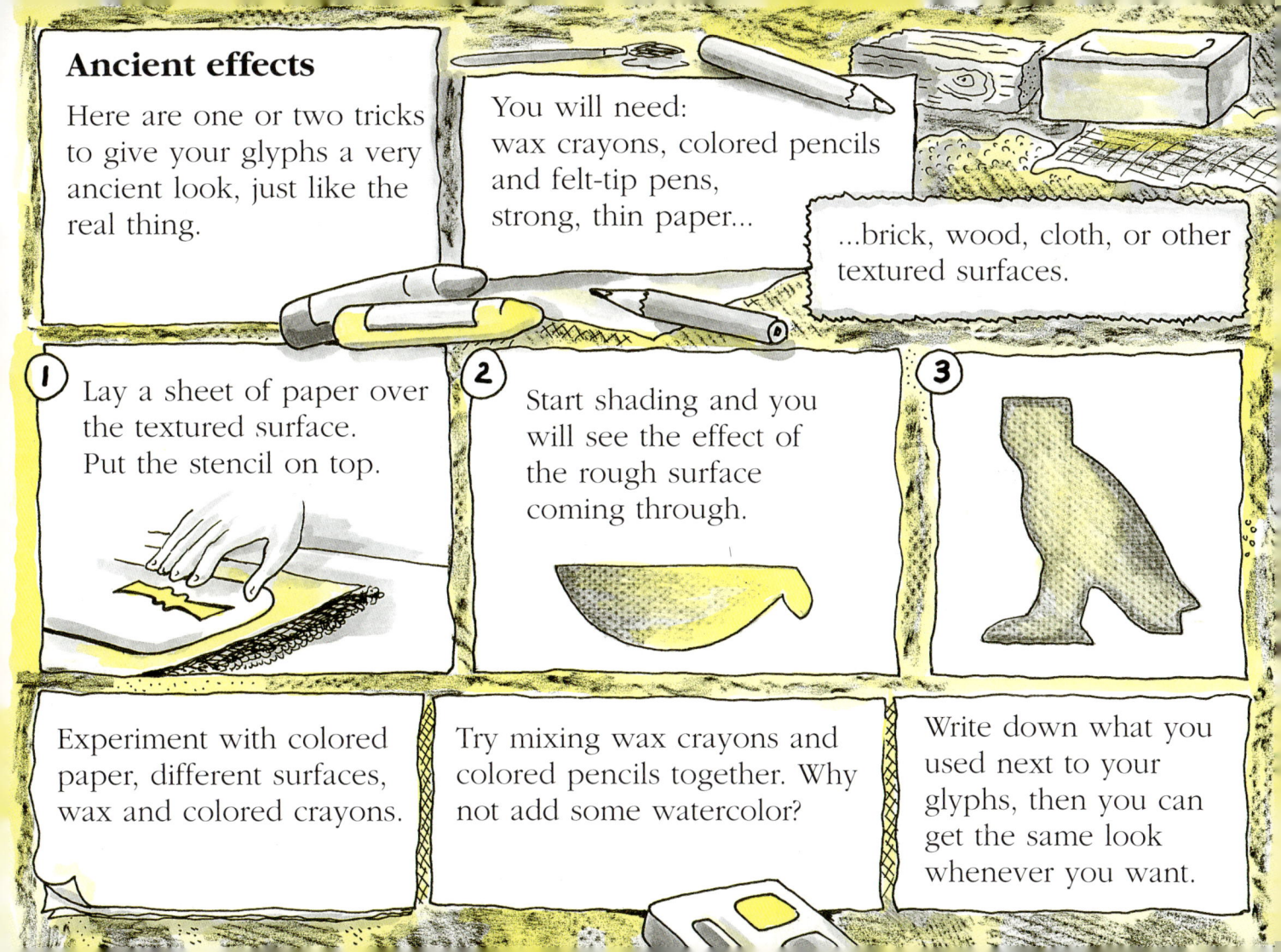

② Start shading and you will see the effect of the rough surface coming through.

③

Experiment with colored paper, different surfaces, wax and colored crayons.

Try mixing wax crayons and colored pencils together. Why not add some watercolor?

Write down what you used next to your glyphs, then you can get the same look whenever you want.

Greeting cards and gift tags

Bored with store-bought cards? Use your stencils on any sort of paper to make a really special greeting card. Try lift-the-flap style with a translation underneath. Everyone will want to be on your Christmas card list!

① CARD
② MEASUREMENTS a+b = c
③ FOLD
④ HIEROGLYPH IT! HERE — CARTOUCHE WITH NAME
⑤ WRITE A TRANSLATION INSIDE — NAME

Your bedroom door

Let everyone know whose room it is with a *Hieroglyph It!* name plate. Stencil your name onto paper, then glue it onto thick cardboard cut in a cartouche shape. Stick it onto your door with double-sided tape. You might have to translate it underneath – not everyone can read Ancient Egyptian!

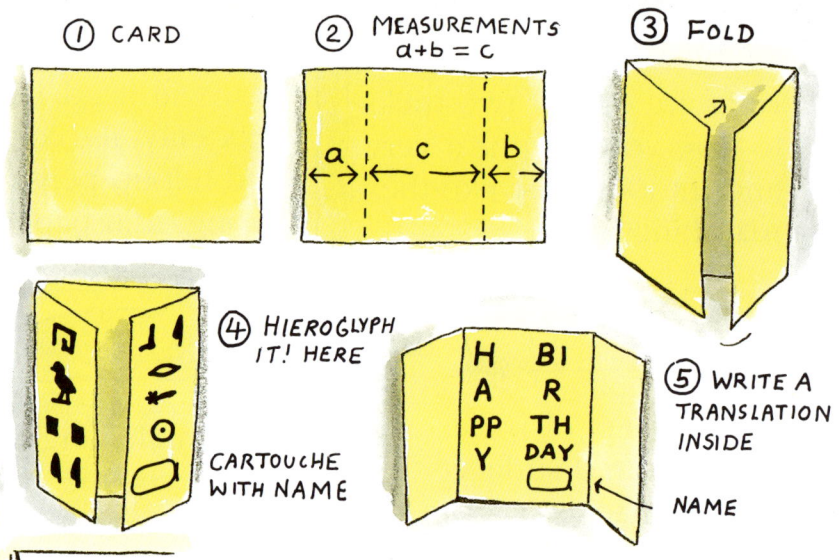

Folders and files

Brighten up dull school files, liven up your old scrapbooks, or finish off a photo album with a new *Hieroglyph It!* cover. Keep your friends guessing with a border made from your favorite star's name.

Only 443,296 shopping days to Christmas.

T-shirts

You will need:
T-shirt (washed and dried if it's new)
fabric paint pens or fabric paint and brushes
piece of cardboard (cereal box)
tape (masking tape is best)
a pencil (special ones that wash out are ideal)

Test out your ideas first by drawing the stencils on a piece of paper and pinning it onto an old T-shirt.

Work on a well-lit, wipe-clean table.

Slip the cardboard inside the T-shirt to stop the paint from going through.

Material doesn't lie flat like paper so gently pull it tight as you tape the T-shirt to the table.

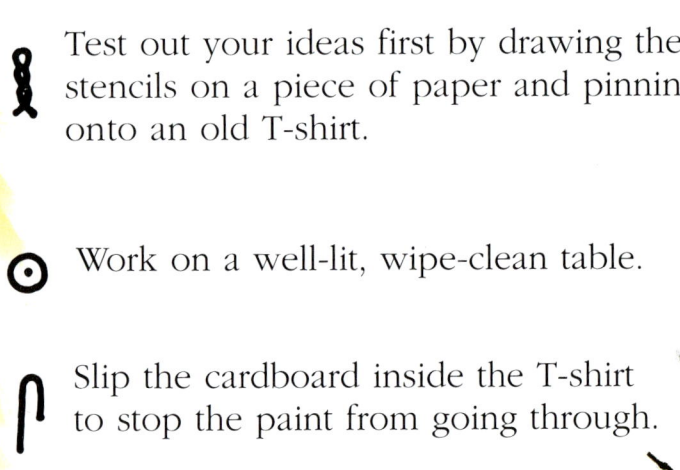

Using your rough copy as a guide, tape the stencil in position and draw the outline in pencil.

Peel off the stencil and tape it again for the next shape.

When you are happy with your T-shirt, put the stencils away. Now you are ready to start filling in the shapes with paint.

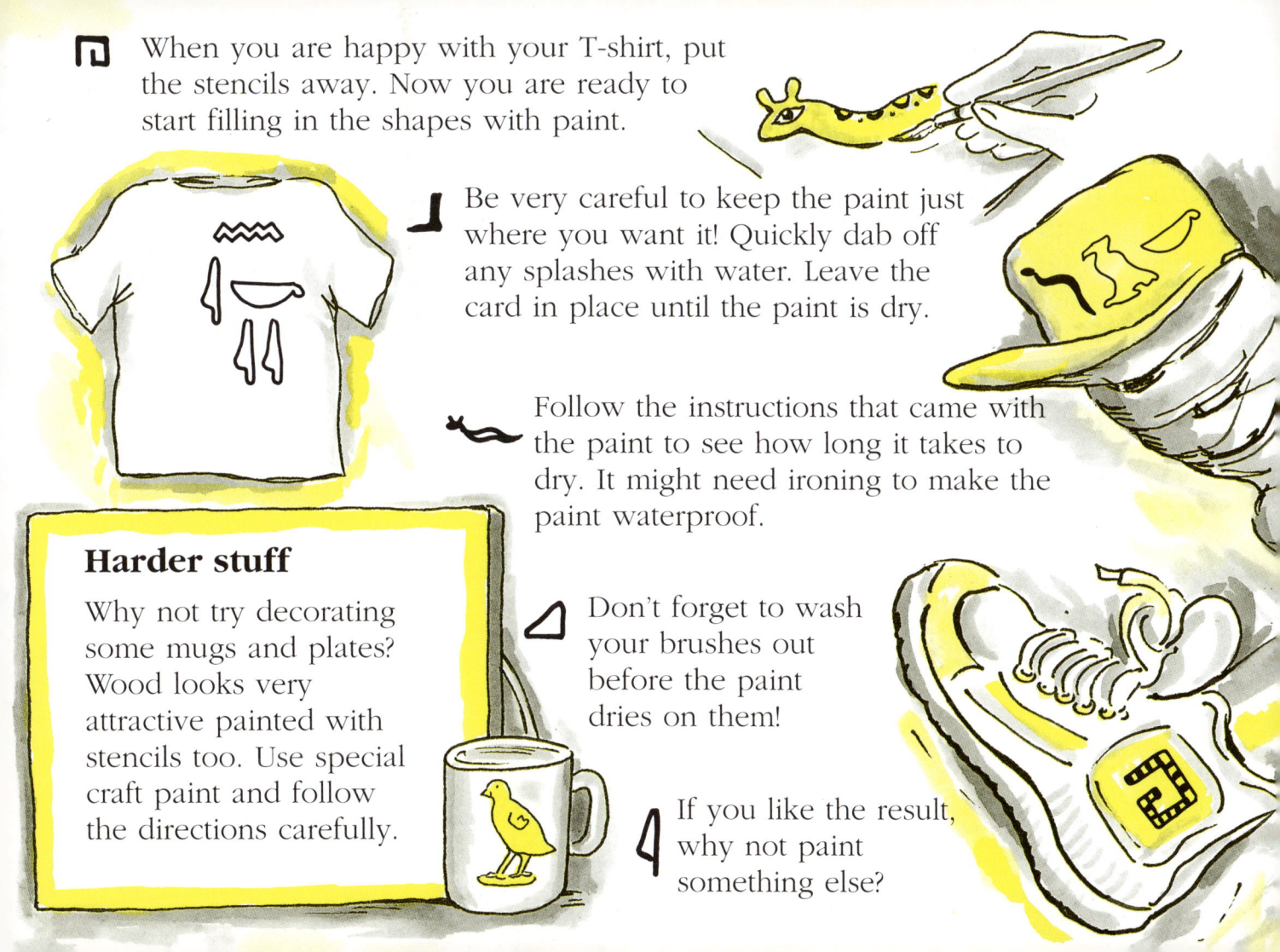

Be very careful to keep the paint just where you want it! Quickly dab off any splashes with water. Leave the card in place until the paint is dry.

Follow the instructions that came with the paint to see how long it takes to dry. It might need ironing to make the paint waterproof.

Harder stuff

Why not try decorating some mugs and plates? Wood looks very attractive painted with stencils too. Use special craft paint and follow the directions carefully.

Don't forget to wash your brushes out before the paint dries on them!

If you like the result, why not paint something else?

Letters and envelopes

Don't just write it, *Hieroglyph It!* Sign your letters with your hieroglyph name and decorate the envelope with a *Hieroglyph It!* postage stamp. For really top secret messages, why not make up a set of your own glyphs with your best friend?

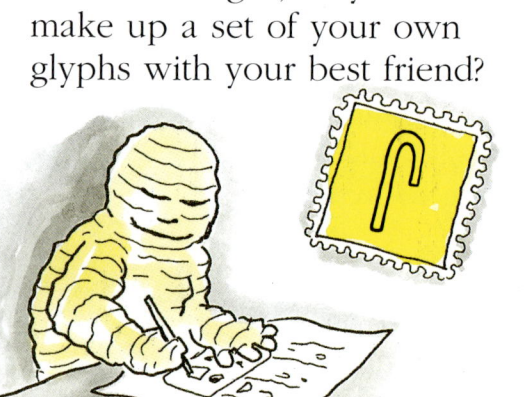

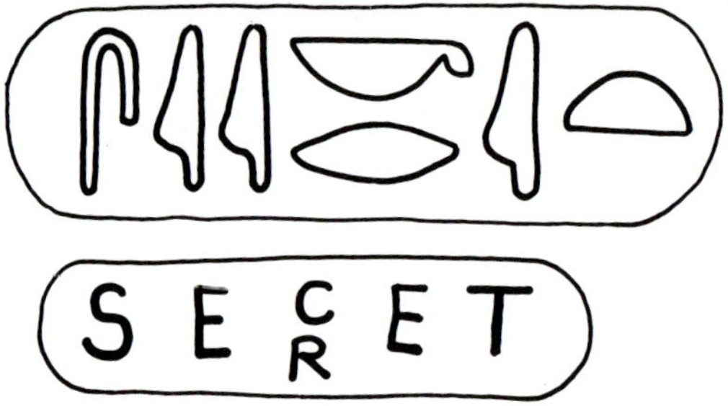

SE{C/R}ET

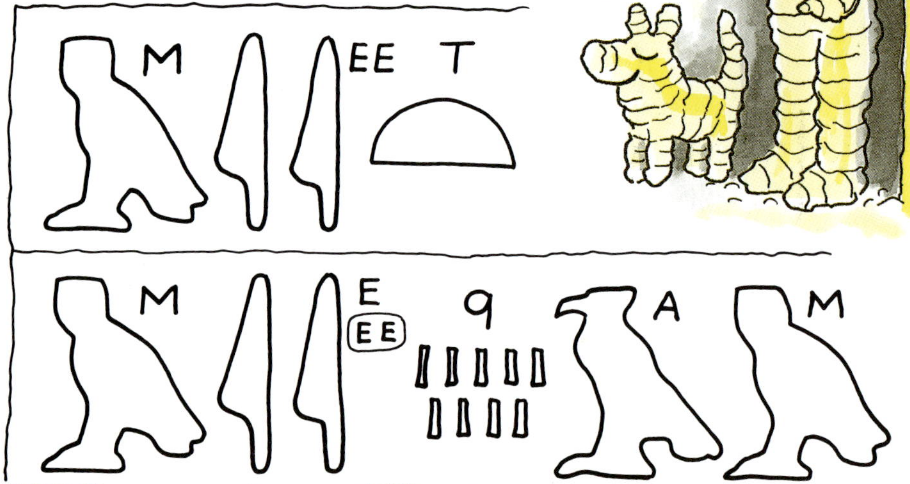

M EE T

M EE q A M

Here are some other important and useful signs.

Seated woman
Used after name (for a female)

Seated man
Used after name (for a male)

| | |

Put after word to make plural

Try writing the hieroglyphs in columns and from right to left, just like the Ancient Egyptians.

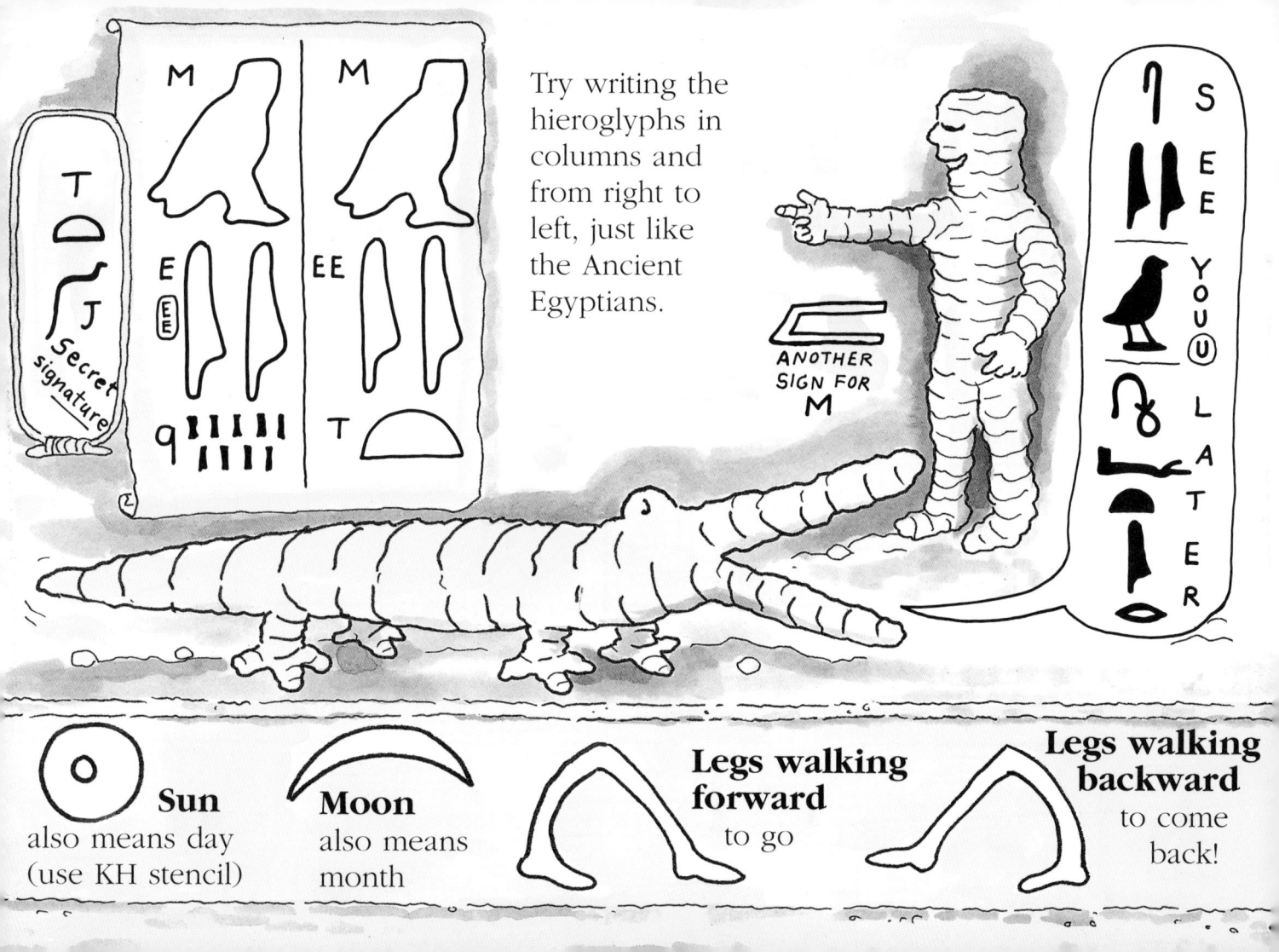

ANOTHER SIGN FOR M

SEE YOU LATER

Secret signature

Sun also means day (use KH stencil)

Moon also means month

Legs walking forward to go

Legs walking backward to come back!

Make up your own picture alphabet. Here's one based on food.

FOODY-GLYPHS for the lips

		d doughnut		i ice cream	
		e egg		j jam	
a apple		f fish		k kebab	
b burger		g gingerbread man		l lemon	
c carrot		h honey		m mushroom	

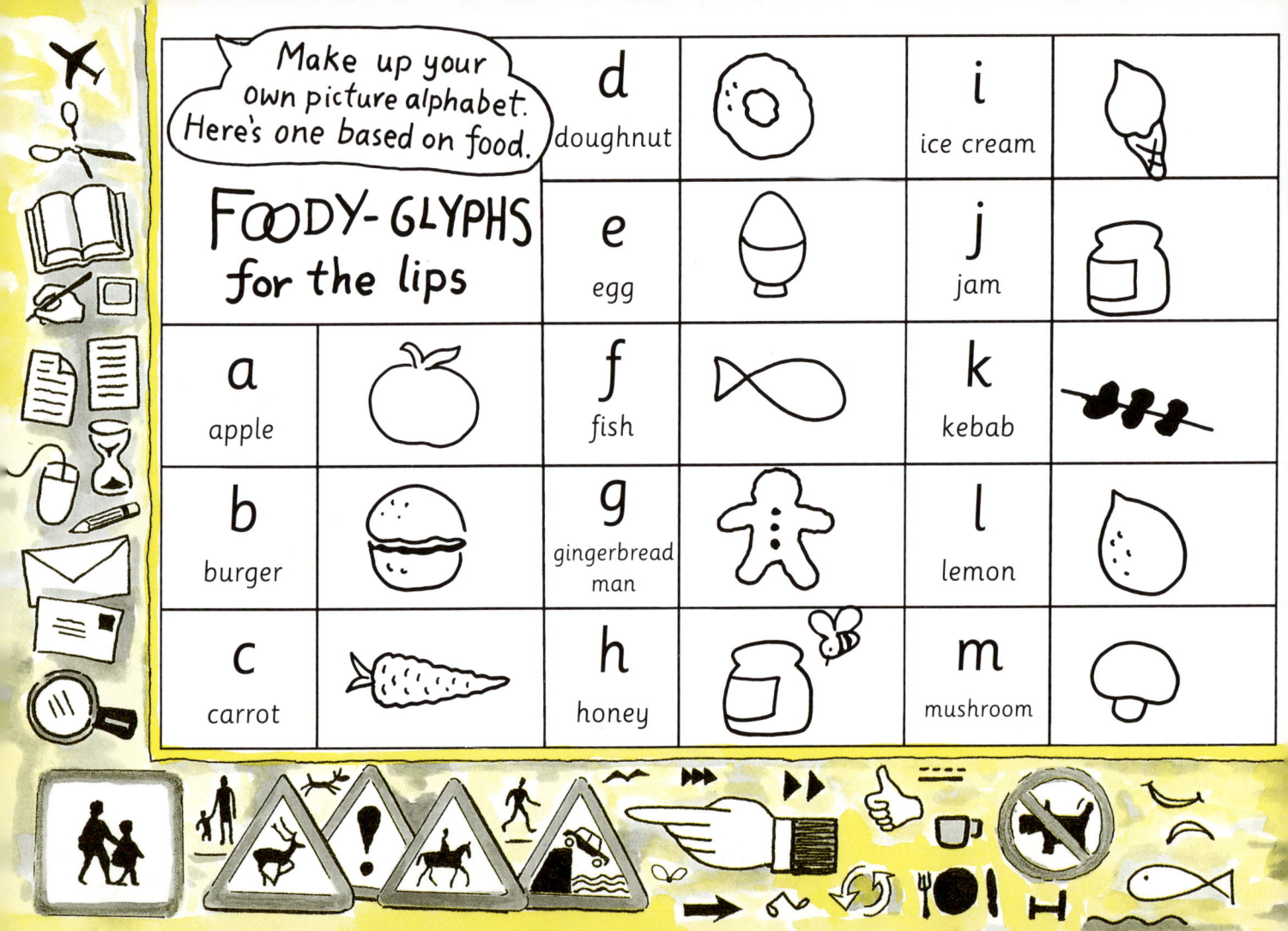

n noodles	🍜	s sandwich	🥪	x extra helping	🍚
o orange	🍊	t turkey	🦃	y yogurt	🥛
p pineapple	🍍	u ugli fruit	☁️	z zits	😮
q quiche	🥧	v vinegar	🍶		*From eating all this food!*
r rice	○○○	w water	🥛		?

Now flip the book over and read all about Ancient Egypt.

Writing English using hieroglyphs

The Ancient Egyptians didn't use vowels (A, E, I, O, U) in the same way as we do in English. To translate English vowel sounds into hieroglyphics you can use:

The vulture for the **A** sounds as in h<u>a</u>t.

The arm for the **A** sounds as in h<u>a</u>te.

The reed signs for the **E** and **I** sounds.

the lasso sign for the **O** sounds.

The quail chick for the **U** sounds.

Don't worry. Nobody knows exactly how Ancient Egyptian sounded.

You can use your stencils and have fun writing English in hieroglyphs, just like a code.

Back cover. It's not a laundry list! It means lord of the throne.

So flip over and find out how to use your stencils.

Hieroglyphs can be read four ways:

1. from left to right like English

if the birds and people face left

2. from right to left like Arabic

if the birds and people face right

Carved and written

Look on the inside of your pack. The hieroglyphs are in two sizes. The larger shows how they looked when carved and painted. The smaller shows how they looked when written on papyrus.

horned viper

F
f

fast
Frank

3. from left to right downward in columns

4. from right to left downward in columns

You'll soon get to know the common glyphs. Then you'll be able to recognize some Ancient Egyptian names and numbers.

KH   U   U

F

Pharaoh Khufu
the builder of the Great Pyramid

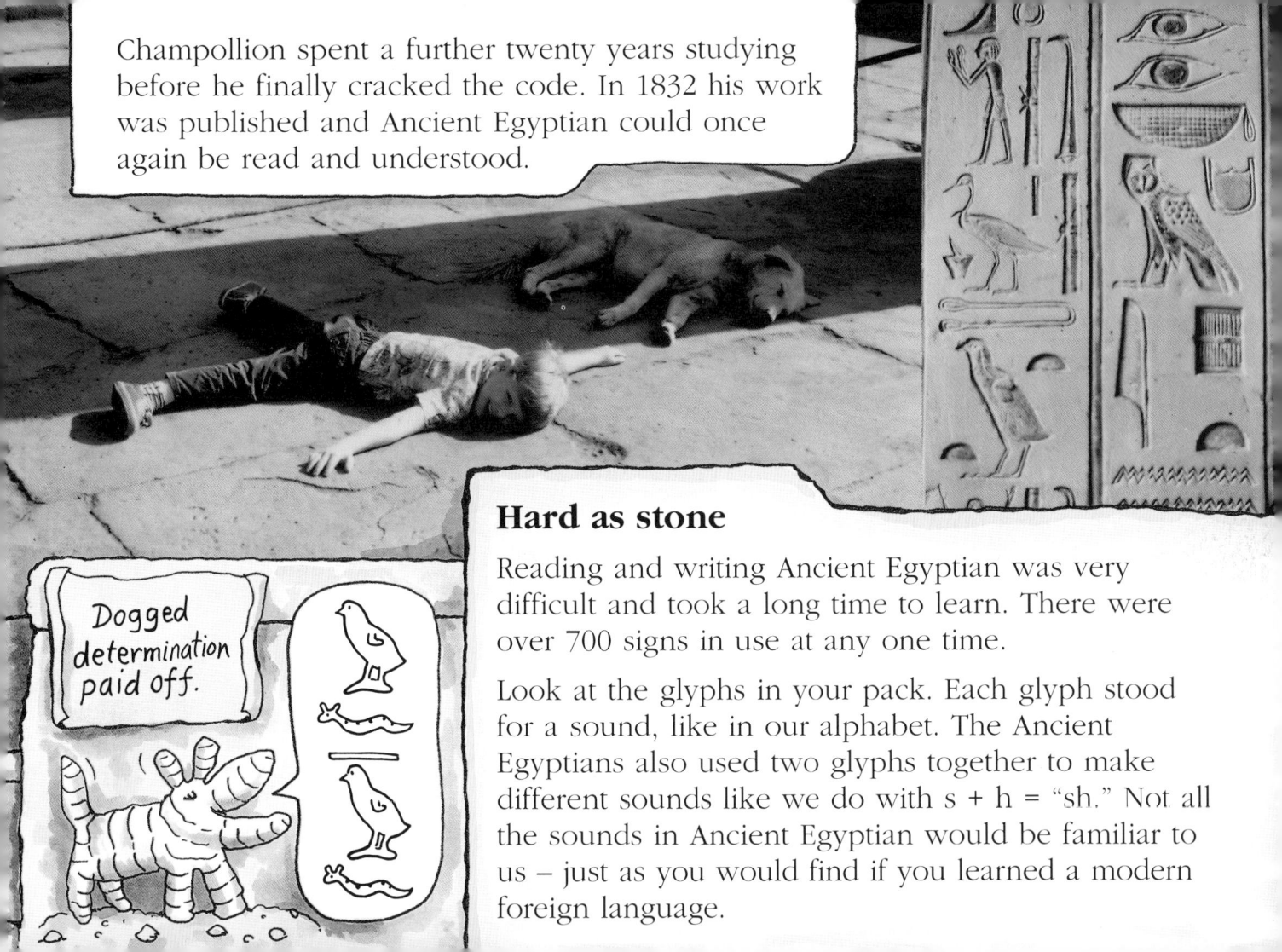

Champollion spent a further twenty years studying before he finally cracked the code. In 1832 his work was published and Ancient Egyptian could once again be read and understood.

Dogged determination paid off.

Hard as stone

Reading and writing Ancient Egyptian was very difficult and took a long time to learn. There were over 700 signs in use at any one time.

Look at the glyphs in your pack. Each glyph stood for a sound, like in our alphabet. The Ancient Egyptians also used two glyphs together to make different sounds like we do with s + h = "sh." Not all the sounds in Ancient Egyptian would be familiar to us – just as you would find if you learned a modern foreign language.

Cracking the code

The Rosetta Stone was studied by two great scholars, Thomas Young and Jean François Champollion. They discovered that hieroglyphs contained in a rope loop (cartouche) were the names of pharaohs. By comparing the names of the Greek rulers, Ptolemy and Cleopatra, to the hieroglyphs in the cartouche, it was discovered that each sign stood for a sound.

C L E O P A T R A

P T O L M Y S

For almost 1,500 years no one could understand it.

It was like someone recording every detail of their life onto videotape and then forgetting how to use the machine.

The Rosetta Stone

Then in 1799, a small slab of stone was found at the mouth of the Nile near the town of Rosetta.

The same message was carved on it in different languages. One was Ancient Greek which they *could* read and one was hieroglyphics.

You can see it in the British Museum in London.

Greeks and Romans

In 332 BC, the Greek emperor Alexander the Great conquered Egypt. Then for 300 years, the country was ruled by Greek pharaohs, all called Ptolemy and Cleopatra. They were followed by the Romans.

The new foreign rulers brought new languages and new religions. The meaning of hieroglyphic writing was lost.

The last scribe?

Tourists have been visiting Egypt for thousands of years. There is a story that about AD 400, a wealthy Roman was on holiday in Thebes. While admiring the already ancient ruins, he was taken to meet a very old man.

This language of birds and plants that is written and carved everywhere— What does it all mean?

I am the last person in the world who can still read it.

Hieratic, Demotic and Coptic

Hieroglyphs, though still carved in temples, were gradually replaced by simpler and quicker forms of writing. First came Hieratic and then Demotic. In the end, Ancient Egyptian was written in Greek with six extra letters for sounds that only Egyptians used. This was called Coptic.

ⲱ ⳃ ⳅ ⳋ ⳡ ⳍ

sh f x h ch g

SPHINX THINK

The Ancient riddle of the Sphinx answer: **man**

4	3	2	1
He crawls as a baby	Uses a stick when old	Walks as a grown-up	

The Coptic Church

All Egyptians speak Arabic now, but there is one link with the speech of Ancient Egypt. The Coptic Christians still use Coptic in their church services today.

The Boy Pharaoh Tut-ankh-amun

In 1922 his tomb was discovered in the Valley of the Kings. It had not been robbed and still contained fabulous treasures of gold and silver.

Written riches

By making lists, scribes could tell the pharaoh just how rich he was and if anyone was stealing from him.

Unless it was the scribe himself!

1,000,000
ONE MILLION

Papyrus to paper

Papyrus reeds grew in clumps along the banks of the Nile. They looked beautiful and were very useful. The Egyptians made them into paper for writing.

Papyrus-making instructions:

Soak the stems in water.

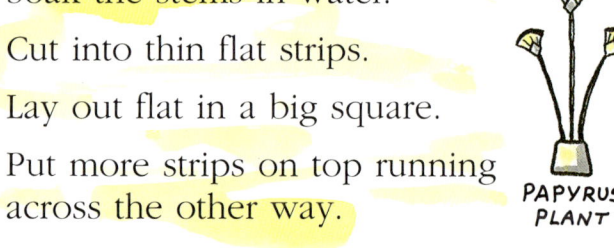

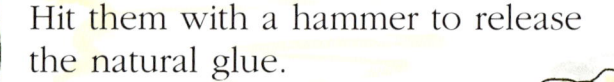

Cut into thin flat strips.

Lay out flat in a big square.

Put more strips on top running across the other way.

PAPYRUS
PLANT

Hit them with a hammer to release the natural glue.

Put heavy stones on top.

When dry, stick the sheets together to make a long scroll.

Nothing is added or wasted.

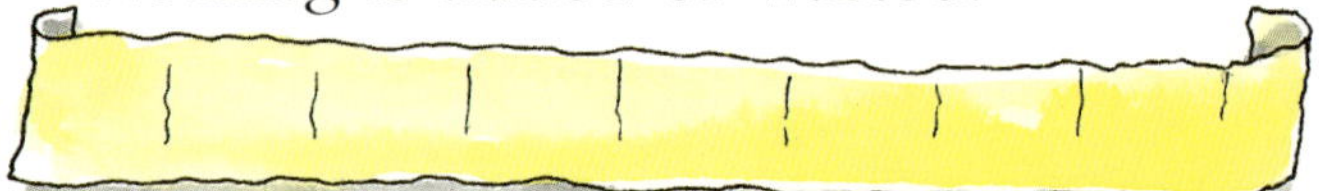

1,350 BC

The boy-king Tut-ankh-amun buried in Kings' Valley or Valley of the Kings (near Luxor).

30 BC

Cleopatra, last queen of Egypt dies.
Egypt becomes part of the Roman Empire.

Scribes

Reading and writing hieroglyphs was very important. Only a few people were allowed to learn. They were called scribes.

WRITING

Mummies

ANKH (LIFE)

The Ancient Egyptians believed in life after death, but only if their bodies were perfectly preserved. These were embalmed and wrapped in linen bandages. The preserved body was called a mummy.

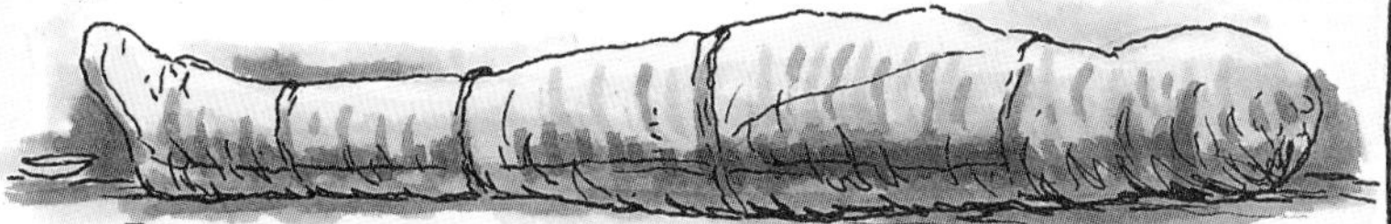

EYE OF HORUS

The ancient riddle of the Sphinx

I say, I say, I say! What has one voice and four feet, then two feet and finally three feet?

Magic meanings

All sacred buildings were covered with pictures and hieroglyphs. The details had to be perfect. In tombs and pyramids they gave instructions for the soul's journey after death.

3,100 BC
Earliest recorded history of Egypt.
Hieroglyphs first used.

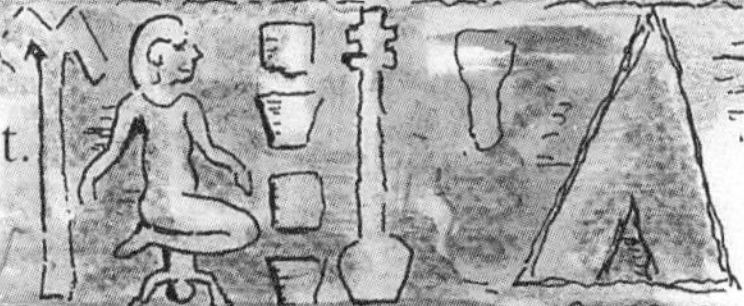

2,700 – 2,400 BC
The Great Pyramids built at Giza
(near Cairo).

The pharaoh

The Ancient Egyptians
worshipped the sun
god Amun-Ra.
The pharaoh was
their ruler. They
believed that he
was not just a king,
but the son of
Amun-Ra himself
– and so did he!

SON OF RA

Message in a battle

ENEMY

Huge battle scenes were carved high
up on temple walls. Hieroglyphs told
how great the pharaoh's armies were and
gave a bloodthirsty warning to their enemies.

The gods

As well as the great
sun god there were
many others.

KING OR GOD

Anubis

He was the dog-headed
god who guarded
the tombs.

Thoth (Ter-hot-eh)

He was the bird-headed god
of writing and knowledge.

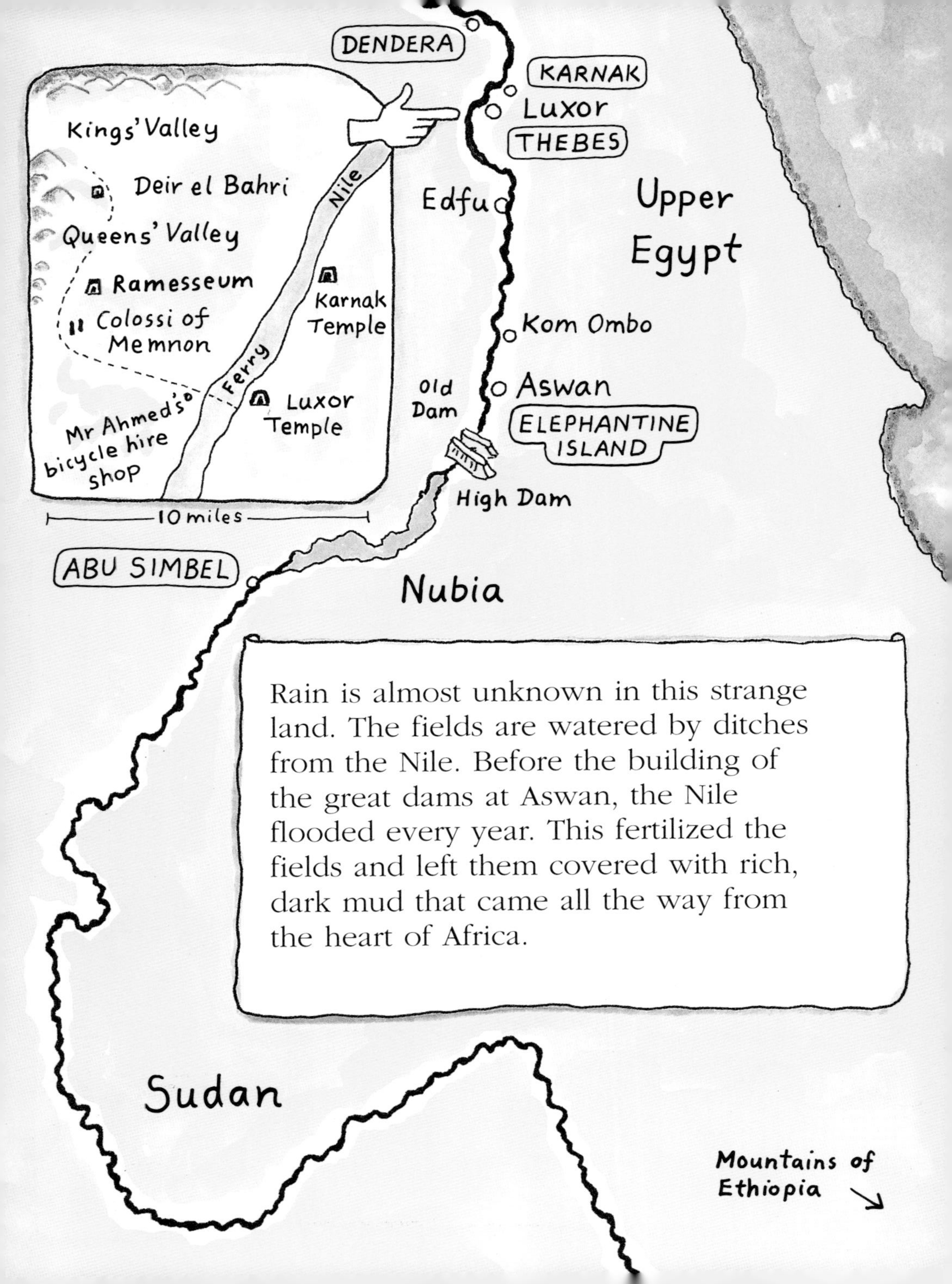

Rain is almost unknown in this strange land. The fields are watered by ditches from the Nile. Before the building of the great dams at Aswan, the Nile flooded every year. This fertilized the fields and left them covered with rich, dark mud that came all the way from the heart of Africa.

Kings' Valley
Deir el Bahri
Queens' Valley
Ramesseum
Colossi of Memnon
Mr Ahmed's bicycle hire shop
Karnak Temple
Luxor Temple
Ferry
Nile
ABU SIMBEL
10 miles
DENDERA
KARNAK
LUXOR
THEBES
Edfu
Kom Ombo
Aswan
ELEPHANTINE ISLAND
Old Dam
High Dam
Nubia
Sudan
Upper Egypt
Mountains of Ethiopia

Egypt is the world's largest oasis. A thin strip of fertile land, it stretches for 744 miles along the banks of Africa's longest river, the Nile. The Ancient Egyptians called their country "the gift of the Nile." The fertile black land by the river they called **Kemi**. The harsh, endless desert which hemmed them in, they called **Desret**, the red land.

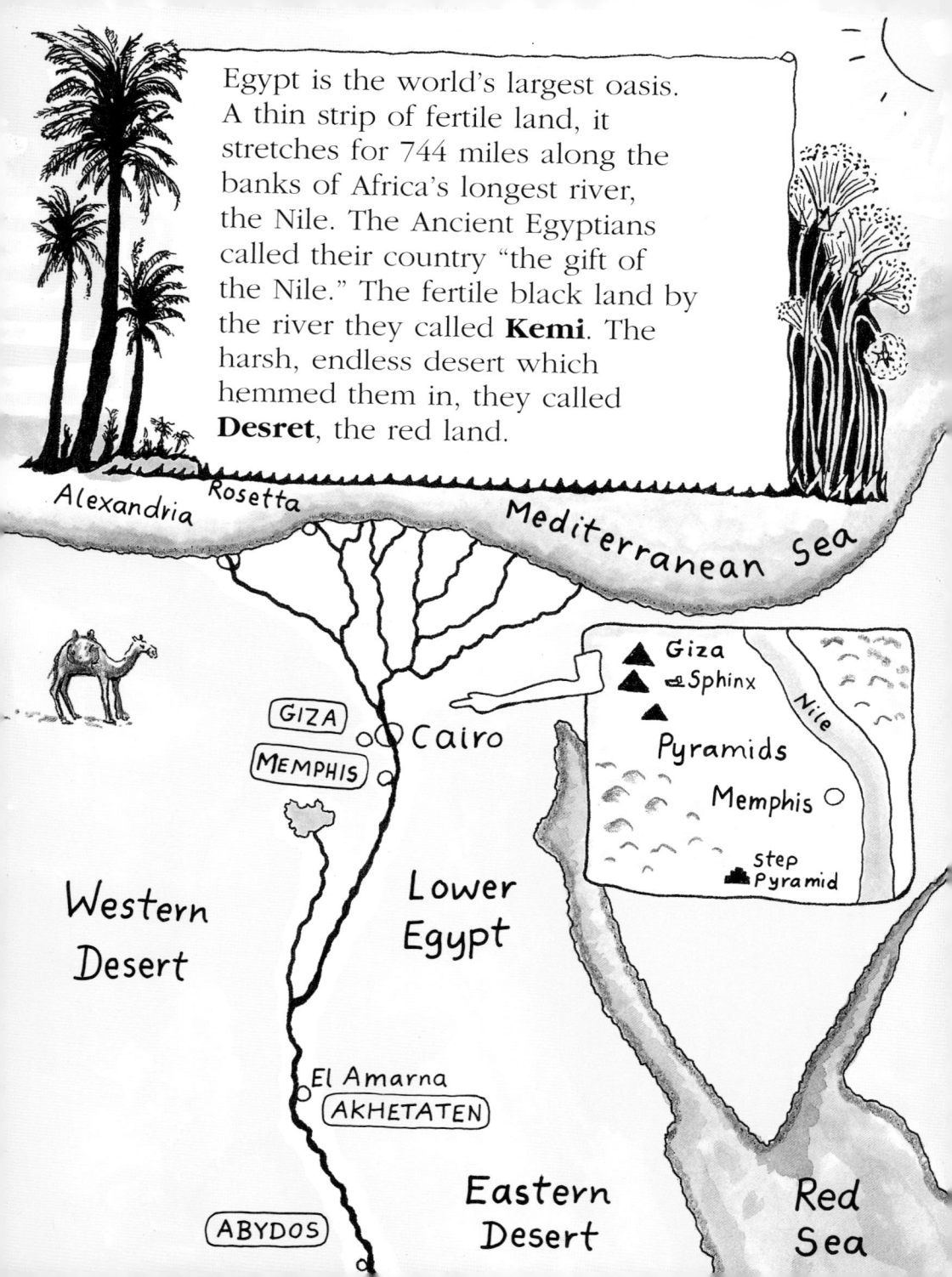

Alexandria
Rosetta
Mediterranean Sea
Cairo
GIZA
MEMPHIS
El Amarna
AKHETATEN
ABYDOS
Western Desert
Lower Egypt
Eastern Desert
Red Sea

Pyramids
Giza — Sphinx
Memphis
Step Pyramid
Nile

| FACTS | ACTIVITIES |

THE SCARAB BEETLE
'KHEPER'
CREATION
AND ETERNITY

DID YOU KNOW?

Egypt

Egypt is a country in Northeast Africa. It was here, over 5,000 years ago, that a great civilization began.

Ancient Egyptians built the pyramids. For thousands of years, they were the largest buildings in the world. Even now nobody can really explain how they were built.

The Egyptians also invented one of the very first written languages – a picture language of beautifully drawn birds and animals – called hieroglyphics.

PYRAMID

HIEROGLYPHIC
The word comes from the Ancient Greek and means
SACRED CARVING